Checklists for Print Media Advertising Planning and Buying

— 13 Basic Checklists —
195 Specific Things to Check When Planning
and Buying Advertising in Periodicals

R. L. Ehler

RICHLER & CO.
Santa Barbara, CA 93105 U.S.A.

0025893

Checklists for Print Media Advertising Planning and Buying
13 Basic Checklists, 195 Specific Things to Check When
Planning and Buying Advertising in Periodicals
by R.L. Ehler

Published by Richler & Co.
754 Palermo Dr. Ste. A
Santa Barbara, CA 93105, U.S.A.
Phone (805) 569-1668
FAX   (805) 569-2279

Copyright © 1997 by R.L. Ehler
Printed in the United States of America

Library of Congress Catalog Card No: 90-63638

Publisher's Cataloging in Publication
(Prepared by Quality Books Inc.)

Ehler, R.L. (Richard Lee), 1930-
    Checklists for print media advertising planning and
buying : 13 basic checklists, 195 specific things to check
when planning and buying advertising in periodicals/R.L.
Ehler.--
    p. cm--(Print media advertising series ; book 4)
    ISBN 1-87929-914-3
    1. Advertising media planning.   2.   Advertising,
Magazine–Handbooks,   manuals, etc.   3.   Advertising,
Newspaper–Handbooks, manuals, etc. I. Title. II. Series

HF6107   659.132
                                          QB90-12
                                          MARC

The Print Media Advertising Series

This book is one of a series published by Richler & Co. The Print Media Advertising Series provides timely, practical information about media planning and buying functions to help the appropriate persons in businesses that advertise as well as those in their advertising agencies.

Books published in this series:

The Print Media Planning Manual: How to Prepare a Media Plan and Buy Space for Periodical Advertising
by R.L. Ehler

Directory of Print Media Advertising Resources: Nearly 400 Sources for Facts and Figures Needed By the Print Media Planner and Buyer
by R.L. Ehler

Media Analysis Tools: For Selecting the Proper Periodicals for the Advertising Schedule
by R.L. Ehler

Checklists for Print Media Advertising Planning and Buying: 13 Basic Checklists, 195 Specific Things to Check When Planning and Buying Advertising in Periodicals
by R.L. Ehler

ABOUT THE AUTHOR

R.L. Ehler has more than 30 years in the marketing communications field, having been at various times in his career an advertising agency co-owner and vice president, account executive, media planner and buyer, copywriter, advertising manager, magazine and newspaper editor, and market planner.

His experience has been on both the agency and advertiser side and covers all media. His articles on advertising planning and media selection have appeared in trade magazines both in the United States and abroad.

His day-to-day involvement with print advertising, complemented by his ability to organize and simplify complex subjects, led him to develop a series of checklists which he could use as a handy reference when preparing media plans and buying space for periodical advertising. He shares these tools with the reader of this book.

TABLE OF CONTENTS

0025893

DISCLAIMER

This book is designed to provide information on print media advertising planning and buying. It is sold with the understanding that neither the publisher nor the author, through this book, is rendering legal, accounting or other similar professional services. If such expert assistance is required, the reader should seek the services of an appropriate professional.

Print media advertising planning and buying are functions that require an investment in time and effort before any degree of proficiency can be achieved.

Every effort has been made to make this book as thorough and accurate as possible. However, there may be omissions or mistakes both typographical and in content. Thus, the text should be used only as a general guide and not as the only source on print media advertising planning and buying. Additionally, this book contains information on the subject only up to the printing date.

The author and Richler & Co. shall have neither liability nor responsibility to any person or organization with respect to any loss or damage caused or alleged to be caused directly or indirectly by the information contained in this book.

WHAT EACH CHECKLIST DOES

1. **Advertising Messages and Media:** Serves as a check on the type of advertising message to be used and the appropriate type(s) of media for the message.

2. **Performing Situation Analysis:** Checkpoints help the media planner understand the situation that has prompted the idea to advertise in the first place.

3. **Budgeting Advertising Expenditures:** Reminds media planner of the space rate and ad production rate considerations involved in preparing a budget and of ways to get the most for the dollars allocated.

4. **Target Audience Input:** Helps in profiling who the target reader is for the advertising message.

5. **Establishing Media Objectives:** Checkpoints cause media planner to structure objectives that are media oriented and measurable.

6. **Developing Appropriate Media Mix:** Causes media planner to consider a "cross selling" media selection approach to satisfying advertising task.

7. **Profiling Media:** Specifies the key factors which need to be examined about each of the contending periodicals.

8. **Performing Media Analysis:** Points out sources for gathering input on contending periodicals and how to treat this input.

9.	**Mapping Media Tactics and Strategy:** Lists media techniques for developing the tactics and strategy needed to wage a competitive advertising campaign.

10.	**Scheduling the Advertising Message:** Guides media planner through the steps involved in scheduling the advertising message for maximum effectiveness.

11.	**Presenting the Media Plan:** Outlines basic content of the media plan in the proper order of presentation.

12.	**Follow-up Action, Monitoring Performance:** Itemizes all the steps that the media planner may be required to take once the advertising has run.

13.	**Conduct of Media Operations:** Traces typical sequential flow of media activities and lists basic media forms.

HOW TO USE THE CHECKLISTS

The checklists serve to remind the media planner and buyer of the important factors that contribute to the development of a comprehensive media program for periodical advertising and to the successful execution of the elements contained in the program plan.

For maximum effectiveness, it is suggested that the lists be used in the order they are presented. This will help the media planner to organize his or her work along the traditional sequence of events.

Read each checklist and each checkpoint within each checklist carefully. You will find that the amount of subject material covered is quite extensive and that the steps the checkpoints require you to take will satisfy virtually all standard print media situations. In addition, they undoubtedly will trigger other ideas for you to consider which are directly related to your particular situation.

You may find that you desire in-depth discussions for some of the checkpoints listed. There are several books available which cover the subject of print media planning and buying. In addition to those listed in the back of this book, you may wish to check with your local bookstore or write to the publishers below for descriptive brochures on their noted books. Publisher addresses may be found in Books in Print at your library.

NTC Business Books, Media Planning by Jim

Surmanek.
NTC Business Books, Essentials of Media Planning by Arnold M. Barban, Steven M. Cristol and Frank J. Kopec.
Arno Press, Scientific Space Selection by Audit Bureau of Circulation, Daniel J. Boorstin-- Advisory Editor.

1. Checklist of Types of Advertising Messages And Media

A. Basic advertising messages.
   Product/service.
   Institutional.
   Classified-recruitment.
   Directory/professional services.

B. Types of print media.
   Consumer magazines--general interest,
      ethnic, class, women's-men's, regional.
   Farm magazines.
   Religious magazines.
   Business magazines--general business,
   industrial, trade, professional,
      institutional.
   Interceptive publications.
   Newspapers--local, regional, national.
   Direct response cards.
   Telephone directories--Yellow Pages, White
      Pages.
   Hybrids--floppy disks■

2. Checklist for Performing Situation Analysis

A. Input derived from interviews with administrative, marketing and sales people at client's house and account management at agency.

B. Structure of <u>written</u> analysis.
Historical look at company product(s) or service(s) as it affects need to advertise.
Present market position defined.
Delineation of problem(s) media advertising is to address as it relates to target audience■

3. Checklist for Budgeting Advertising Expenditures

A. Method for arriving at budgeted amount.
   Task method.
   Percentage of sales.
   Combination of above.

B. Space rate considerations.
   Typical magazine page increments--1/6, 1/4,
      1/3, 1/2, 1/2 island, 2/3, full page.
   Bleed charges--usually 5-10% of black and
      white rate.
   Common newspaper formats--broadsheet,
      tabloid.
   Standard Advertising Unit (SAU)
      measurements.
   Four basic categories of Yellow Page
      advertising space--listings, trademarks
      and trade names, space ads, display ads.
   Full press run, split run, geographic and
      demographic editions, day of
      (newspaper) appearance.
   Special position, insert charges.
   Circulation as the basis for the advertising
      rate.
   Local versus national rate for newspapers.

C. Ad production rate considerations.
   Publication repro material requirements.
   Different sizes among publications.

Costs associated with ad production--layout, photography, model fees, location fees, photo retouching, type, photostats, mechanical assembly, color separations, negatives, reprints, agency markups.

D. Ways to maximize advertising dollars.
Rate protection.
Multi-divisional corporate rate.
Combination buys.
Rate holders.
Two percent cash discount.
Remnant space.
Investing in ad message enhancement--page size, color, unusual ad format, placement on page.
Rates based on inquiries pulled.
Agency guaranteed results.
Rate negotiating.
Merchandise aids.
Buying space at net.
Media buying service■

4. Checklist of Target Audience Input

A. Discipline/occupation.
   Type of engineer, scientist, doctor, lawyer, architect, artist, musician, teacher, journalist, etc.

B. Job function
   Design and development (equipment), engineering services (e.g., evaluation, QC, reliability, standards, test), basic research, manufacturing/production, etc.

C. Title
   President, chairman, owner/partner, vice president, manager, superintendent, foreman, group leader, etc.

D. Industry
   Standard Industrial Classification number.

E. Prospect level (product/service stage)
   Original equipment manufacturer (OEM), fabricator, systems manufacturer, distributor, wholesaler, end user.

F. Geographic location
   Global region (e.g., Europe, Australasia, Latin America); country; region (e.g., Mountain, Pacific, New England); state;

county; area (e.g., ADI, DMA, MSA, primary market area, retail trading zone, city zone); city.

G. Population
   Age, sex, race.

H. Income
   Personal, household.

I. Social structure
   Level of education, religion.

J. Factors affecting buying patterns
   Hobbies, fashion trends, seasonal aspects, price/budget availability, approval process, etc.■

5. Checklist for Establishing Media Objectives

A. Structure the wording of the objectives to address media activities only.

B. Express objectives in quantitative, measurable terms.

C. Action tools for quantifying objectives.
   Reach.
   Frequency.
   Gross Rating Points.

D. Report on performance in meeting objectives■

6. Checklist for Developing Appropriate Media Mix

A. Marketing input required.
   Product/service to be advertised.
   Markets to be addressed.
   People within markets.
   Tasks assigned to advertising.

B. Characteristics desired in media to be considered.
   Timeliness of issuance.
   Compatibility of editorial format: News? Tutorial? Reference?
   Media appropriateness to complexity, length, etc., of advertising message.

C. Need for different types of media based on makeup of target audiences, location of target audiences, multi-media support requirements.

E. Need for medium within medium for multiple exposure impact■

7. Checklist for Profiling Media

A. Frequency of issue.
   Directories--annual, semiannuals.
   News-Feature publications--bimonthlies,
      monthlies, biweeklies, weeklies, dailies.
   Non-feature new product tabloids--
      bimonthlies, monthlies.

B. Date established.
   Age as a measure of stability and standing
      in market served.
   Start-ups--for covering unfilled market
      needs, new emerging markets, or simply
      for publisher's own gains?

C. Location of editorial offices.
   Pertinence of editorial headquarters
      location to center of market activity.
   Existence of field offices.

D. Editorial thrust.
   Statement that 1.) defines market
      segment(s) covered and 2.) details types
      of editorial material published.

E. Physical size of publication.
   Physical size of advertising units available
      are contingent on size of publication--
      potential effects on production cost,

cost of space.

F. Total circulation.
   View total figure as only one aspect of
   circulation.

G. Paid vs. free and non-paid controlled
   circulation.
   Major strengths of paid circulation--larger
   passalong readership; more in-depth
   editorial.
   Major weaknesses of paid circulation--
   usually less circulation; doesn't deliver
   the breadth of a field.

H. Audited vs. non-audited.
   Audited statement--advertiser's independent
   (non-publisher) assurance that
   publication will deliver its
   claimed market audience.
   Only two reasons for considering a non
   audited publication--1.) non-existing
   audited alternative--e.g., new publishing
   venture, 2.) audit is pending.

I. Selective circulation buys.
   Geographic.
   Demographic.
   Metro.

J. Foreign circulation.
   Organized by country within international
   regions.

K. Newspaper circulation analysis.

Geographic breakdown (city, retail trading and primary market zones; ADI and DMA).

Market makeup (number of households, gross household income, number of men and women, age, etc.)

L. Industry/business/SIC circulation.
Number of readers by product/service activity.
Number of readers by U.S. Government classification
(SIC) of economic activity.

M. Job function circulation.
By occupation and by title.

N. Ad makeup by product/service.
Number of ads by unit size run during past six or twelve months on same product/service as advertiser's.

O. Editorial makeup by product/service.
Number of editorial pages run during past six or twelve months devoted to advertiser's product/service.

P. Editorial awards.
Good writing, good reporting equals best read publications.

Q. Editors with pertinent degrees.
Pertinent education and work experience helps editors perform their editorial duties.

R. Reader service card return inquiries processed.
Total from all issues published during past
year.
Total by general product or subject
category.
Total ad inquiries compared to total
general editorial inquiries.
Personal experience with past track record.
Direct advertiser contact via toll free 800
number in ad as an alternative to bingo
card.

S. Cost per thousand.
A quality product should carry a quality
price.
Question unusually low cost per thousand
rates.

T. Competition's use.
Take competition's use as signal to ask
yourself why it uses the publications it
does.■

8. Checklist for Performing Media Analysis

A. Circulation statements.
   Source of subscription request as an
      indicator of intent to read.
   Subscription by individual name has most
      worth.
   Be wary of 20 percent or more non-
      qualified non-paid circulation.
   Are ad rates charged in line with
      circulation delivered?
   Number of subscribers paying full
      subscription rate.
   Affect of premiums (if used) on
      publication's readership.
   Subscription turnover rate.
   Ratio of non-paid to paid subscriptions
      over time.

B. Publisher's sworn statement.
   Question validity of submission of
      publisher's sworn statement if the
      non-audited publication is more than
      6 or 12 months old.

C. Editorial considerations.
   In what way(s) is the publication written to
      attract the readership of its subscribers?
   Total the number of pages devoted to each
      editorial category and compare with

competing publications.

The more focused the editorial the higher the readership.

Determine and tabulate articles by source of editorial input (senior editor, junior editor, contributed, etc.).

Ascertain level of editor's knowledge and experience and correlate with bulk of editorial being published.

D. Audience simulations.

Simulated reader projections should be considered second choice to actual measurement in arriving at circulation profile.

E. Added research input.

Magazine page exposure (MPX) and Ad Sightings.

F. Media evaluation format.

The key publication factors for measuring and comparing on weighted and non-weighted basis (see previous checklist).

G. Judgement calls.

On established publications--check distribution outlets. Study editorial-- does it fit with readers claimed?

On start-ups--check out the business premise■

9. Checklist for Mapping Media Tactics and Strategy

A. Know the publication "terrain" on which to wage your ad campaign as well as what competition is doing.

B. Intelligence gathering.
Via magazines' space salesmen.
Via analysis/tracking services.

C. Franchise positioning.
Franchised paid positioning (usually 10 percent of black and white rate.
Positioning on request (as available) at no charge.
No-no's--no color ad on same page; no competition on same (or even facing) page; no uncomplimentary editorial on same or facing page.

D. Scheduling considerations.
Advertising should follow publicity.
Factor seasonality of product/service.
Time new product announcements around availability of product.
Coordinate (as appropriate) advertising appearance with magazine trade show issues.
Allow enough time for production/coordination of special ads such as pop-ups.

Complement advertising presence/volume
with product's use/availability during
year.

E. Inserts and outserts.
Value of inserts rests with their onetime
impact.
Outsets provide faster, cheaper means of
distributing catalogs, etc., than
traditional bulk mail route.

F. Combination buys.
Use different types of media in concert
(media synergy) to build on ad message
delivery and impact.

G. The advertorial allows for comprehensive
presentation of message.

H. Exotic ads are ultimate (and most costly)
vehicles for dramatizing advertiser's
messages.

I. Demographic ads allow for very specific reader
penetration■

10. Checklist for Scheduling the Advertising Message

A. Scheduling for events.
   Allow ample time for ad material
   production and shipment.
   Check on space closings well in advance.

B. Publicity timing.
   Coordinate advertising appearance plans
   with publicity appearance plans so that
   product exposure occurs over as long a
   period of time as possible.

C. Editorial calendars.
   Use as a guide in scheduling advertising so
   that it appears with complementary
   editorial.

D. Schedule sheet contents.
   The schedule sheet should encapsulate all
   pertinent information concerning the
   advertising buy including cost, date of
   appearance, ad headline, ad size, closing
   data, researched issues.

E. Guidelines for achieving adequate prospect
   contact (business to business) per ad subject
   while taking advantage of opportunities to
   achieve cost effectiveness with the advertising
   dollars available:

Frequency--minimum of five insertions (single ad message) in each magazine; 15 in newspapers.

Recall--concentrate appearances of each ad message in as tight a time frame as possible (e.g., in monthlies, minimum every month for five straight months).

Repeatability--loss of ad copy readership power is a very slow process.

Inquiry response--will hold up fairly well over the insertions and much of what is lost can be replaced with a program of postcards in combination with the display space schedule.

Media spread and duplicated readership--concentrating the ad schedule in the top two to three publications will prove to be the most cost effective and provide the most unduplicated readership.

Ad economy--prepare only the number of different ads that can be run according to the above guidelines ■

11. Checklist for Presenting The Media Plan

A. Detail parameters (as follows) observed in developing media plan.
   Situation analysis.
   Target audiences.
   Annual print media budget.
   Marketing objective(s) to be addressed.

B. Present itemization for each of the basic highlights (presented below) that form the outline of the media plan.
   Salient features.
   The case for print media.
   Media advertising (objective(s).
   Media strategies.
   Publication profiles & rationale for selection.
   Scheduling tactics.
   Ad placement tactics.
   Merchandizing.
   Budget allocation.
   Appearance schedule■

12. Checklist for Follow-up Action, Monitoring Performance

A. Tear sheets/complementary copies.
   Carefully check these to assure ad insertion compliance in addition to proper editorial environment.

B. Make goods.
   It is the media buyer's responsibility to request these, in writing and in a timely fashion.

C. White space.
   If not cancelled in time, agency-advertiser is responsible for payment of space ordered. Publication is under no obligation to find a substitute buyer for the space.

D. Return of materials.
   It is the advertiser's responsibility to request return of ad materials.
   Publication will destroy them after one year from last use.

E. Short rate.
   If you use less space than what is required by the per insertion rate originally agreed to, you will owe the difference between the contracted rate and rate

actually earned.

F. Rebate.
   If you ran more space than you had
   contracted for, a payment (based on
   lower rate earned) is due you.
   Don't wait for publication to offer.
   Claim it.

G. Rate protection (against future increase).
   There is no such thing. However, the
   advertiser may cancel at time change in
   rate becomes effective without incurring
   new rate adjustment provided old
   contract rate has been earned up to
   date of cancellation.

H. Billing.
   Agency/client becomes obligated to cost of
   space on space closing date even
   though media bill may not be due and
   payable until 20-30 days after
   publication. If agency's client will not
   pay on advanced billing, some means of
   assuring funds will be available to
   agency must be devised!

I. Inquiry counts, processing.
   Instruct publication on where to send
   inquiries resulting from advertising.

J. Readership scores.
   Use as measure of effectiveness of
   preferred positioning, ad size, color in
   addition to creative power.

Request copy of research report summary
from your space salesman■

13. Checklist for the Conduct of Media Operations

A. Typical sequential flow of media activities.
 Investigate and write situation analysis for media plan.
 Determine target audience.
 Set media objectives.
 Perform media analysis.
 Develop media tactics-strategy.
 Engage in negotiations with publications.
 Make media selections.
 Place media orders.
 Follow-up on tearsheets/comp copies, make goods, short rates, rebates, rate changes, billing instructions, readership checks, return of materials.
 Make inquiry processing arrangements.

B. Basic media forms.
 Media insertion requisition.
 Advertising insertion order.
 Agency media invoice.

C. Establishing credit.
 Bank references.
 Reference other publications in which advertising placed.
 Initial payment provisions■

CHECKLIST OF MEDIA TERMS

ADI--Area of Dominant Influence.

Agate Line--A unit of advertising space measurement equal to 1/14 inch in depth by one standard column in width.

Benday--A process for adding shaded or tinted areas made up of dots for reproduction by line engraving.

Black and White Page--A full page advertising unit which employs black ink on white stock.

Blackjack Advertising--A ploy sometimes used by media salesmen whereby editorial space is promised in return for an advertising contract. Advertisers have also been known to attempt this tactic only in reverse.

Blanket Contract--An agreement between an advertiser and a publication which covers all products advertised, regardless of the agencies or advertiser's divisions or subsidiaries involved.

Bleed Ad--An advertisement whose illustration or inking goes to the edge of the page on one or more sides.

Census Audit Report-- An analysis of the number of plants and establishments in the field covered by the publication, reported by state or other geographical area, and by one or more of the following: type of business, size, volume and/or number of employees.

Circulation--The total number of distributed copies of a publication at some specific time.

Combination Rate--The rate, often discounted, for advertising space in two or more periodicals under one ownership. Also a special rate granted advertisers who run in both morning and evening editions of a newspaper.

Contract Year--A contractual relationship between publication and advertiser lasting 12 months from the placement of the first of a series of advertisements.

Controlled Circulation--Distribution of a periodical to a preselected readership at no charge.

Cost Per Thousand--The cost per 1000 readers delivered by a publication.

Demographic Edition--A special edition of a publication directed to a specific audience makeup.

DMA--Designated Market Area.

Double Truck--An advertisement running across a pair of facing pages in a publication--sometimes referred to as a spread.

Duplication Audit Report--An analysis of duplicate circulation among publications published by a single firm in regard to business/occupational and geographical breakdowns of qualified circulation.

Duplication--The same number of people, households or companies reached by two or more publications.

Extension--Additional time granted to the advertiser by the publication beyond the normal material closing date in which to supply the required ad materials.

Flat Rate--The base rate not subject to frequency or quantity discounting. Also called open rate.

Flighting--To alternate active and inactive periods of advertising; to intersperse the appearance of advertising over a period of time; results in concentrated periods of ad appearances.

Four-Color Page--A full page advertising unit which employs the standard 4A colors (yellow, red, blue, and black) each by themselves or in any combination thereof.

Fractional Space--Advertising space measuring less than a full page; usually referred to for the smaller units in magazines--e.g., 1/6 or 1/9 page.

French-Door Gatefold--An advertising insert in a magazine which has the paper folded toward the vertical middle on both sides.

Frequency Discount--A discount on the regular rate granted to the advertiser for running a certain number of ads in a given period.

FSI--Free Standing Insert made available by newspapers.

Gross Rating Point--The product of media reach times exposure frequency.

Insert--An advertisement printed separately from the periodical that is bound with or tucked into its regular pages; usually printed by the advertiser, then shipped to the periodical for insertion; generally printed on special stock or with special color that is superior to that of the rest of the periodical.

Island--An advertising position on the page that is completely surrounded by editorial matter; normally available only in newspapers.

Junior Page--An advertisement size whose dimensions qualify it as a full page in standard size magazines but which is only a partial page in over-sized magazines such as tabloids. When run as a junior page, editorial matter appears on two to four sides of the advertisement.

Leading--The amount of space used between lines of type. A lead is a piece of metal 1/36th of an inch (2 points) thick. Six point leads or larger are called slugs or quads.

Make Good--The rerun of an advertisement to make amends for faulty reproduction or for failure to present the advertisement as ordered.

Material Closing--The date by which the advertiser must submit repro or photographs, copy and layout to the publication to satisfy the space insertion order.

Milline--One agate line appearing in one million copies of a publication.

MPX--Magazine Page Exposure. A measurement of the number of times a reader sees a page in a magazine. The page may contain editorial and/or advertising. When combined with other data--such as number of people exposed to ad, reading time, primary audience, place of reading--the MPX technique provides a good estimate of potential audience the space buyer can expect from a given magazine. A comparable technique to MPX is Ad Sightings.

MSA--Metropolitan Statistical Area.

Non-Qualified Circulation--Recipients who do not meet the publication's definitions of the field served and recipient qualification. Advertiser and agency copies fall into this category. Non-qualified recipients are not included in the effective coverage or in determining advertising rates.

Off The Card Rate--A special advertising rate, usually negotiated, which is not shown on the printed rate card.

Open Rate--See Flat Rate.

Open Rate--The maximum rate charged by a publication.

Pass-along Readership--The number of persons other than the original subscriber or purchaser who read an issue of a publication.

Penetration--The degree of effectiveness in reaching a target audience.

Per Inquiry Rate--A publication's rate for advertising space based on the number of inquiries pulled by the advertisement.

Pica--A unit of type height equal to 1/6 of an inch; 12 points equal one pica.

Point--A unit employed in measuring the height of typeset; equal to 1/72 of an inch (1/12 of a pica). Thus, there are 72 points to an inch. Type in sizes below 18 points is generally considered body type, while more than 18 points is considered headline type.

Pop-Up--An advertisement bound in the center of the magazine and which features die-cut construction so that when opened a part of the advertisement rises from the page.

Preferred Position--A location for an advertisement in a publication that is considered to offer enhanced readership--e.g., page opposite table of contents, outside back cover, inside front cover, center spread, etc.. A premium rate is charged for these positions.

Primary Market Zone--Area in which the newspaper publisher considers the newspaper has its greatest strength on the basis of readership and editorial coverage.

47

Pulsing--See Flighting.

Qualified Circulation--Circulation based on readership eligibility.

Qualified Circulation--Circulation for which the publication has documentary evidence of the recipients mailing address, evidence that the person meets the definitions of the field and occupations served, is correctly classified by business/occupation breakout of circulation and has received the publication for a minimum of six months.

R.O.P.--Run of paper; position ad anywhere in publication.

Rate Holder--A small advertisement placed to earn a frequency or quantity discount; usually run when larger size units are not scheduled for appearance; a means of maintaining "presence" in the publication, although its primary function is to earn or protect the frequency or quantity discount.

Reach--Percentage of people or households who are exposed to an advertising message over a period of time.

Rebate--A payment made by the publication to the advertiser when the latter's advertising volume exceeds the contractual commitment. The amount is based on the lower rate earned.

Remnant Space--Unsold space in the final page makeup of a publication. Because the sale of the space had been anticipated, the cost of the space is discounted in an attempt to find a last minute buyer. Generally is sold through a space broker.

Scotch Print--A reproduction proof which shows all color proofed in black.

Selectronics™ Ad--A patented (R.R. Donnelly & Sons Co.) binding and imaging process which permits specially encoded signatures of a publication to be printed with subscribers' names

48

and personal messages addressed to those subscribers. This computer-directed printing and mailing process personalizes each subscriber's issues by modifying the different ads and editorial pieces with geographic, even reader profiles such as the individual reader's names.

Short Rate--The difference between the contracted rate and the rate actually earned.

Space Closing--The date by which the advertiser must commit/contract for the rental of space in a given issue.

Spadeos--The small wrappers around the edges of Sunday newspaper sections.

Split Run--Publication of two different pieces of copy in the circulation of a magazine so that no one reader is exposed to both messages. A technique commonly used for testing ad copy.

Spread--See Double Truck.

Supplementary Audit Report--A detailed analysis of the buying authority or influence of a publication's recipients or an analysis of the number of secondary or multiple products, functions and titles of the qualified recipients of a publication.

Supplement--A separate publication which is included with the standard editorial section of a newspaper--e.g., the Sunday supplement, Parade Magazine.

Tabloid--A newspaper of less than standard size, usually 11 1/2" wide by 15" high.

Till Forbid--A media insertion order term meaning run this ad till forbidden or told to stop.

Unit Audit Report--An analysis of the number of plants and establishments a publication reaches, broken down by geographical area and one or more of the following: business, occupation, title, function, volume of business and/or number of employees.

White Space--The result of not getting ad materials to the magazine in time to meet its material deadline or press deadline--in effect, paying for black or white space in the issue in which an insertion was ordered but for which the repro material was lacking.

INDEX

A

B

C

D

E

F

G

I

J

M

N

O

P

Q

R

S

T

W

FOR MORE INFORMATION

Print media planning books by R.L. Ehler.

Print Media Planning Manual--A complete practical guide to preparing a media plan and buying space for periodical advertising. Takes the reader step by step through the media processes including [] finding direction for the planning process [] budgeting expenditures [] negotiating with periodicals [] targeting the right audiences [] setting appropriate objectives and measuring performance [] using different media in one plan [] profiling competing periodicals [] sources for media facts and figures [] analyzing pros and cons of each medium [] mapping tactics and strategies [] scheduling ad appearances [] presenting the media plan [] following through after placement [] trade customs and practices [] organizing a media operation [] media terms and their definitions.

Directory of Print Media Advertising Resources--A comprehensive directory listing the names, addresses and telephone numbers of virtually every important source for facts and figures about periodicals, organizations and services--both in the United States and abroad--which are available to the print media advertiser, planner and buyer. Extensive description of resource content/service provided also included for most listings.

Media Analysis Tools--A set of tools that allow the advertising media planner to systematically measure and compare on a numerical basis the various attributes of competing periodicals in a given advertising situation. These tools can be an indispensable aid to making sound decisions concerning media selection since they allow the media planner to examine the most crucial aspects of a publication's worth to the advertiser.

Checklists for Print Media Advertising Planning and Buying--13 basic checklists, 195 specific things to check when planning and buying advertising in periodicals. These handy checklists cover all of the considerations that the media planner needs to make when preparing a media plan and buying space for periodical advertising.

Request FREE descriptive brochure from Richler & Co.

ORDER FORM

RICHLER & CO.
754 Palermo Dr., Ste. A
Santa Barbara, CA   93105 U.S.A.
Phone (805) 569-1668
FAX   (805) 569-2279

Please send me the following books by R.L. Ehler

___copies of Print Media Planning Manual @ $49.95 ea.
___copies of Directory of Print Media Advertising
Resources @ $44.95 each.
___copies of Media Analysis Tools @ $34.95
___copies of Checklists for Print Media Advertising
Planning & Buying @ $19.95 each.

Ask about quantity discount rate.

I understand that I may return any book for a full refund
if not satisfied.

Name_____
Address_____
_____Zip_____

Californians: Please add 7.75% sales tax.

Shipping: $2.00 for the first book and 75 cents for
each additional book.

_____I can't wait 3-4 weeks for Book Rate Shipment.
Here is $3.50 per book for Air Mail

ORDER FORM

RICHLER & CO.
754 Palermo Dr., Ste. A
Santa Barbara, CA 93105 U.S.A.
Phone (805) 569-1668
FAX (805) 569-2279

Please send me the following books by R.L. Ehler

___copies of Print Media Planning Manual @ $49.95 ea.
___copies of Directory of Print Media Advertising
Resources @ $44.95 each.
___copies of Media Analysis Tools @ $34.95
___copies of Checklists for Print Media Advertising
Planning & Buying @ $19.95 each.

Ask about quantity discount rate.

I understand that I may return any book for a full refund
if not satisfied.

Name_____
Address_____
_____Zip_____

Californians: Please add 7.75% sales tax.

Shipping: $2.25 for the first book and $1.00 for
each additional book.

___I can't wait 3-4 weeks for Book Rate Shipment. Here
is $3.50 per book for Air Mail